SMILEY
A JOURNEY OF LOVE

JOANNE GEORGE

Fitzhenry & Whiteside

Published in Canada by Fitzhenry & Whiteside, 195 Allstate Parkway, Markham, ON L3R 4T8
Published in the United States by Fitzhenry & Whiteside, 311 Washington Street, Brighton, MA 02135

Fitzhenry & Whiteside acknowledges with thanks the Canada Council for the Arts and the Ontario Arts Council
for their support of our publishing program.

We acknowledge the financial support of the Government of Canada through
the Canada Book Fund (CBF) for our publishing activities.

Library and Archives Canada Cataloguing in Publication

George, Joanne, author
Smiley : a journey of love / Joanne George.

ISBN 978-1-55455-412-6 (hardcover)

1. Service dogs--Juvenile literature. 2. Golden retriever--
Juvenile literature. 3. Blind dogs--Juvenile literature. I. Title.

HV1569.6.G46 2017   j636.7   C2017-903360-3

Publisher Cataloging-in-Publication Data (U.S.)

Names: George, Joanne, author.
Title: Smiley : A Journey of Love / Joanne George.
Description: Markham, Ontario : Fitzhenry & Whiteside, 2017. |Summary: This is the inspiring story of a "special needs" dog
rescued and nurtured by the author who found that he was uniquely suited to serve as a therapy dog.
Identifiers: ISBN 978-1-55455-412-6 (hardcover)
Subjects: LCSH: Animal welfare – Juvenile literature. | Dogs with disabilities – Juvenile literature.
| BISAC: JUVENILE NONFICTION / Animals / Animal Welfare. | JUVENILE NONFICTION / Animals / Dogs.
Classification: LCC SF992.D46G467 |DDC 636.70886 – dc23

Cover and text design by Tanya St. Amand

Printed in China by Sheck Wah Tong Printing Press Ltd.

I would like to dedicate this book to my dad,
Victor Whiteley, who taught me that every life matters,
and to the late Dr. Ralph Watt, DVM, for whom
I worked from the time I was fourteen years old,
and enabled me to help so many animals.

CHAPTER ONE

SMILEY, THE THERAPY DOG

A warm smile is the universal language of kindness.

William Arthur Ward

Smiley is a Golden Retriever. He was born in a puppy-mill in Ontario, Canada. Smiley was born without eyes and with a genetic condition called "dwarfism." Dogs with dwarfism may have a larger than normal head, a deformed jaw with a shorter nose, crooked teeth, and short legs that might be bowed or twisted. Dogs with dwarfism often have enlarged joints.

Smiley came into this world with the odds stacked against his survival. But Smiley was lucky. He did survive. He even became famous. This is his story.

Joanne George, a veterinary technician from Stouffville, Ontario, rescued Smiley from a puppy-mill. Joanne and her associates at the vet clinic had been assigned to inspect the mill to determine the living conditions of the dogs housed there. It was a cold wintry day in February 2004 when they went to investigate.

WHAT iS A PUPPY-MiLL?

Most of us know that a mill is a factory where consumer goods are made to be sold.

A puppy-mill is a factory, too, but in a puppy-mill, the workers are dogs who are bred over and over to produce puppies. The more puppies produced and sold, the greater the profit for the mill owner. Newborn puppies, as young as five weeks old, are taken from their mothers and sold to pet shops, flea markets and even over the Internet. These puppies are likely to have health problems because of the puppy-mill conditions. Often, these concerns are of no importance to the mill owner, whose ultimate goal is to produce as many puppies as possible for the least amount of money. Puppy-mills are a million-dollar business.

Parent dogs in a puppy-mill do not fare any better. They are kept in tiny, cramped cages or, alternatively, all together in large pens. These dogs are not fed nutritious food, and often they do not have clean water. When several dogs are herded together in a big area, the weaker dogs starve, or can be hurt in fights. Another hazard is weather exposure — heat stroke in summer, freezing conditions in winter. It is not likely a vet will be called should puppy-mill parent dogs or their offspring have bad teeth, an injury, or become ill.

Unless they are lucky enough to be rescued, these dogs will probably not survive.

Smiley was born and grew up in such a place, until he was rescued....

When Joanne first saw Smiley, his ears were split and he had fresh wounds on his face. "The smell in that barn was horrible, but none of the dogs wanted to leave because that was the only life they knew. Each dog we were able to rescue had to be carried outside and placed into crates in the back of my dad's pickup truck, which he had lent to me hoping we would be bringing home some lucky animals. These were the injured, the old, and the unwanted dogs, but, ultimately, they were the lucky ones. Each dog we saved was bathed, neutered or spayed, and adopted into a wonderful forever home."

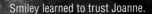
Smiley learned to trust Joanne.

There is nothing impossible
to him who will try.

ALEXANDER THE GREAT

Joanne admits the first few days were a bit of a blur after she brought Smiley home. She already had a partially deaf Great Dane who was eager to pounce on any new dog. Joanne was certain that this new, frightened, dwarf-sized Golden Retriever would be better off and feel much safer in another home without other dogs. Joanne's co-workers persisted, however,

Joanne soon learned from Smiley that nothing would move forward without practice and patience.

insisting that she take Smiley. "For some reason, they knew he belonged with me," and finally, Joanne agreed to foster the small Golden Retriever until a permanent home could be found for him.

Joanne's earliest memories of Smiley were of him curled up tight, as small as he could make himself, in corners of the house. She would find Smiley under the end table beside the couch, or behind the door in the kitchen, or as far back as he could get behind the television. Smiley also wedged himself in behind the sofa, where he chewed on the leather. All the electrical cords in his hiding places were soon gnawed to bits. "This little yellow dog was truly suffering inside, and he chewed on everything around him as a result." So the cords were spliced back together and the couch remained as is until Smiley was healed of his anxieties.

Joanne soon discovered that nobody wanted to adopt an untrained dog with special needs. Six months passed, and Smiley was rejected over and over again. All the other Golden Retrievers rescued that wintry day had been adopted into loving homes. Only

> **Keep your face always toward the sunshine—and shadows will fall behind you.** WALT WHITMAN

Smiley was left. Finally, Joanne understood that Smiley was her dog, and that he would be happiest living with her.

Smiley did not do well when left alone. Joanne discovered that whenever she put Smiley in a crate to keep him safe while she was out of the house, his anxiety level increased. Joanne would come home to find him covered in his own feces; he often injured himself trying to escape the close confines. "Smiley will just have to come with me everywhere," Joanne decided. And so he did.

Initially, Smiley did not enjoy riding in any vehicle. "So, every morning, before going to work, I would get up fifteen minutes earlier, and try to persuade Smiley to jump into the SUV. He panicked if I picked him up. I realized that he needed to trust me, and to trust himself...and he had to make this adjustment on his own. I could help him, but I could not do it for him. Otherwise, if I just put Smiley somewhere, he would not really know where he was, or how he got there, and that was not fair."

Joanne soon learned from Smiley that nothing would move forward without practice and patience. She taught herself to remain calm when she was rushed and when things got stressful. "Once I understood how Smiley needed things to be, we were both more at ease. Soon Smiley was trotting off leash from the front steps of his new home to meet me at the car door. He taught me self-control, understanding, and acceptance."

As she watched and concentrated on Smiley's demeanor, Joanne discovered that his empty eye sockets were causing discomfort. The eyelashes had retracted inwards into the empty spaces where the eyeballs should have been, creating considerable irritation and pain. Joanne took Smiley to a vet, who advised that the eye sockets be totally cleared of all tissue, then permanently sewn shut, in what would be major surgery. Dr. Kevin Isakow, a leading Toronto veterinary surgeon, offered his services. The procedure took two

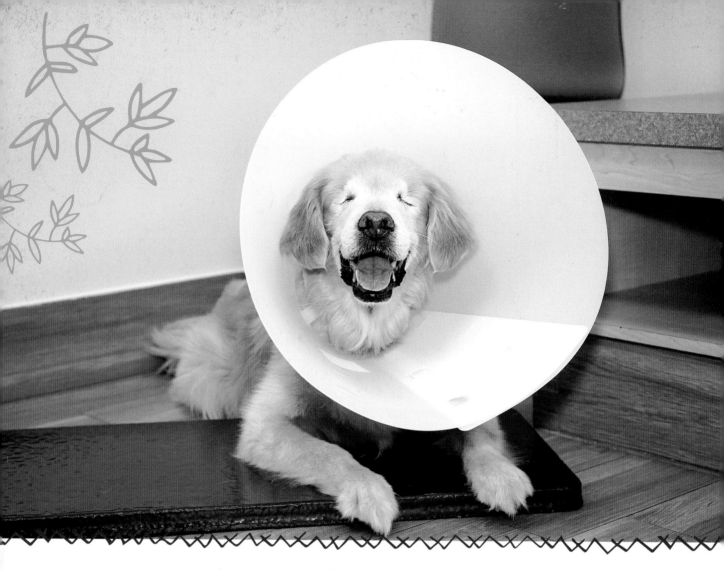

hours. The result: Smiley suddenly had a whole new look. His perpetual smile would not only change Smiley's life, but the lives of everyone this special dog would come to meet.

After surgery, Smiley had to wear a neck cone. This plastic collar prevented him from scratching at his eyes, re-opening incisions, and further scarring his face. Smiley's anxiety seemed to lessen after his operation, and Joanne soon felt that some of his behavioural issues had been the result of the eye pain. Smiley wore the neck cone for a full four weeks after his surgery and during that time, Joanne discovered yet another amazing facet of her new dog. Smiley "sees"

the world through sound. When he wore the cone, it filtered sound like a tunnel. The only noises Smiley could hear came from directly in front of him. He could not even follow Joanne's voice as she moved around a room. Once the cone was removed, however, Smiley could retrieve a ball thrown from anywhere, because he followed its sound from initial toss to landing thud.

Smiley also relies on his acute sense of hearing both to navigate and to track the events around him.

Smiley's hearing acts like sonar, or even like the echo-location used by bats. Smiley uses sound to locate himself within his

surroundings, and Joanne thinks he can even hear himself walking. When Smiley passes a parked car, or other similarly large object, he will turn toward it, sensing possible danger.

It is easy to forget that Smiley cannot see. These days he goes about life as any other dog might, padding along confidently, head held high, when he and Joanne are out for a leash walk around town. Sometimes Joanne takes her whole dog family (Smiley, plus two Border Collies) on a leisurely stroll. Smiley is a happy member of the pack. The people who stop Joanne to ask

Smiley goes about life as any other dog might, padding along confidently, head held high.

about Smiley's lack of eyes are astounded to see a blind dog strutting so proudly down Main Street, Stouffville, amid all the fuss and commotion.

Even though she is a dog trainer, Joanne herself often forgets about Smiley's disability. When working with her canine students, Joanne teaches hand signals with each verbal command. As her students progress, she moves solely to hand signals. Every once in a while Joanne finds herself using these hand signals with Smiley, even though he cannot see them. "I think what anyone with a disability wants is to be treated as if there were no disability... I think they wish that people would forget about what they cannot do and value what they can do. So, no, I don't feel silly for forgetting that Smiley cannot see – I think that's what he wants."

Whoever is happy will make others happy too.

ANNE FRANK

CHAPTER TWO

SMiLEY AND JOANNE

Disability is a matter of perception. If you can do just one thing well, you're needed by someone.

Martina Navratilova

Smiley on a country road. Pure canine bliss!

Joanne began Smiley's training the moment she lifted him into her father's truck. It was Joanne's job to make sure that Smiley's new life was a fun and positive learning and growth experience. Joanne believed that the most important thing she could teach Smiley was self-confidence, how to be a regular dog. Every time she introduces Smiley to a new situation or experience, Joanne is careful to ensure that he understands everything is going to be okay.

At one point, Joanne and Smiley lived in an apartment. Each night Smiley would jump onto her bed and snuggle. Both would sleep like babies until morning.

Joanne knew that Smiley had never been in a car before she

rescued him. She worried about the effect the car noise, its vibrations, the trauma of getting in at one place, and out at another, a new location with different sounds and smells, would have on Smiley's confidence. And, initially, she was right to worry. Smiley was stubborn. He did not like the car but Joanne persisted. She would tap, tap, tap on the floor inside the car, saying "up, up, up...." The process would be repeated, over and over and over again, until finally, Smiley would jump in. Once adjusted, Smiley rapidly became an expert at judging the exact height of his transport. He could even make it into the back of a pick-up truck on a single leap.

One thing that totally amazes Joanne is the fact that, like most other dogs, Smiley knows where he is going in the car even before they arrive. He gets excited when he feels the first pothole on the laneway into the barn where Joanne keeps her horse. That bump means an afternoon of romping with other dogs, playing in the tall grass, an occasional snack of manure balls, and perhaps a long trail ride. A long gravel road means off-leash hiking in the forest, and a three-hour drive means several days of pure canine bliss at the cottage.

Joanne introduced Smiley to "cottage life" shortly after he recovered from his eye operation. Although it is a well-known fact that Golden Retrievers love water, they need to become acquainted with the concept of swimming at an early age. Smiley had never been to a lake. He had probably never had a bath, but the first time Joanne took him north,

Golden Retrievers have an instinctive love of water, and are easy to train to basic or advanced obedience standards. The Golden Retriever is popular as a disability assistance dog such as being a guide dog for the blind and a hearing dog for the deaf. The breed's friendly, gentle temperament has also made it the third-most popular family dog breed (by registration) in Canada and the United States.

Golden Retrievers love the water and are good swimmers.

he was ready. Smiley was intrigued by the new scent of water the moment he jumped from the truck. With tail waving like a flag, Smiley wandered down the steep hill to the shoreline. The lake's smell and sound seemed to trigger his instincts as a retriever. It was a magical moment for Joanne as she watched this little puppy-mill dog's instincts guiding him. Initially, Smiley jumped back in surprise when the cold water first touched his toes; then he ran forward to another wave, and to the next, and then to still another. Finally, Smiley waded out into the water. As it rose higher and higher up his body and finally up to his neck, Smiley began to swim...doing what Golden Retrievers have long been bred to do.

Although Smiley was adjusting well to his new life, he remained very unhappy when left alone. When Joanne's employer said Smiley could come to work with her, Joanne seized the chance. And now, every morning after breakfast, Smiley sits by the front door, waiting for Joanne to get ready. And every day at the vet clinic, Smiley snoozes under the front desk. Whenever the front-door buzzer sounds, Smiley gets up to greet the new patients and their families. His happy, gentle demeanor always seems to calm even the most stressed-out visitors.

The bond that links your true family is not one of blood, but of respect and joy in each other's life.

RICHARD BACH

Smiley lives with two hyper-active Border Collies, Pearl and Pippi. They are very intelligent but they are always running around the house, and they both keep bumping into the closed glass doors leading into Joanne's backyard. Smiley hasn't hit the glass once. He knows when the doors are open, and when they are closed; he can feel the drafts, and he can smell the outdoors. Smiley is the only one of Joanne's dogs who never steps in a mess — because of his increased sense of smell. Pippi is a faithful friend to Smiley. She seems to sense his special needs. She doesn't mind when Smiley follows the smell of food right to her bowl, and she makes sure he does not lose the scent trail on any hike through the woods.

Smiley's family, Shepherd, Joanne, and Darrin

CHAPTER THREE

SMiLEY & JOANNE'S NEW FAMILY

Family is not an important thing. It's everything.

Michael J. Fox

Joanne and Smiley had been together for four years when Joanne married Darrin George in 2008. Smiley shared the day with his family and was very much a part of the ceremony, just as Joanne had dreamed he would be. Smiley wore a gold bowtie and a white shirt collar, and carried a little pillow with the two wedding rings on it up the aisle.

When Joanne found out she was going to have a baby, she wondered how her dogs would react, and, more specifically, how Smiley would react. He had never had any experience with infants. Joanne had visions of the baby crawling over to a soundly sleeping Smiley, pulling his ears, grabbing his nose, and screaming and crying. What would Smiley

do? Luckily, Joanne had nine months to read about babies and dogs, and how best to bring the two universes into harmony. "All of the dogs must have sussed out the fact that something special was going on," she noted "because when we brought baby boy Shepherd home in June 2009, not one dog raised a whisker."

To Smiley, the baby was a new scent, and Smiley kept his distance. Gradually, as Shepherd grew, Smiley began to move closer and closer, beginning to feel more comfortable with this newest member of the George pack. Joanne took all three dogs for daily "pack walks," and all three proudly pranced along beside the baby carriage. This was no easy task because the stroller with the baby scent rolled straight and fast, over toes, knocking the dogs sideways should they venture too close. "That baby was all business, and demanded respect," Joanne said... "and he got it."

"Do I have special dogs or an exceptional child?" Joanne would ask herself. Now she believes she was blessed with both.

Many Smiley fans ask whether Smiley is always as happy as he seems. His tail never stops wagging. He reacts to the positive attitudes of his people. Joanne is careful never to be sad or negative in Smiley's presence because Smiley would share her sadness. "He would be nervous in new environments, and not attempt things on his own if I did that," she says. Even when Smiley bumps into objects around him, his tail continues to wave. Joanne does not run to comfort him when one of these accidents happens. Instead she uses an animated voice, "Whoopsie" or "Uh-oh!" Smiley's tail keeps swinging, and he turns to the sound of Joanne's tone.

One new innovation in Smiley's life was the introduction of a large stuffed toy that Joanne gives to Smiley every time he finds himself in an unfamiliar place. Smiley, like any Golden Retriever, proudly carries the toy around in his mouth. Should he bump into an object, the soft plush acts as a buffer. When the toy hits a wall, Smiley knows it is time to change direction.

Sometimes Smiley explodes with excess energy, but he does not zip crazily around the house the way many dogs do. Perhaps he knows he could get hurt. Instead, Smiley will choose a spot in the middle of the living room and spin, and spin, and spin, and spin. When his energy is drained, Smiley will flop down like a rag doll, grinning and panting, justifiably proud of the show he has put on for his family. Smiley is capable of almost anything any dog can do, but he's smart enough to know his limits.

Smiley and Shepherd,
the best of friends

No act of kindness, no matter how small, is ever wasted.

AESOP

CHAPTER FOUR

ST. JOHN AMBULANCE THERAPY DOGS

Memories of our lives, of our works and our deeds will continue in others.

Rosa Parks

Soon after rescuing Smiley, Joanne began to think about how his unique talents might be used to help others in need. "I knew that one day he would make a wonderful therapy dog. Smiley visited my grandmother several times in her nursing home. She loved to see him, and really enjoyed his presence. I noticed that other residents as well also found joy in watching Smiley stroll down the hall on the way to Grandma's room. He always knew exactly where it was. It was the seniors I met in the nursing home, and all the people who would stop by to hear Smiley's story, that made me search for an organization that would help Smiley work with the people who needed him most."

Several years later, while out for a walk with her dogs, Joanne was again suddenly brought face to face with the remarkable effect Smiley has on people. A woman stopped to ask about Smiley, listening to his story while she crouched and rubbed her cheek on the top of

When dogs fulfill their roles they are ecstatically happy.

ROBERT CRAIS

his head. Joanne and the woman talked for a bit, then the woman hugged Smiley and thanked Joanne for rescuing him. Some six weeks later, while on another walk, Joanne and Smiley met the woman again. She came running up to them and, putting her arms around Smiley, told Joanne she hadn't been able to stop thinking about him since their first meeting. She had been having a really tough time, and Smiley had inspired her to get through it. Although Joanne had known about Smiley's "healing powers" for years, this chance meeting reaffirmed her goal of having Smiley tested to be a certified therapy dog. "I was going to share Smiley with as many people as I could."

WHAT iS A THERAPY DOG?

Therapy dogs provide comfort to people in emotional distress or isolation. They work alongside their handlers to make affectionate contact with unfamiliar people in sometimes stressful environments. The most important attribute of a therapy dog is its temperament. Good therapy dogs have a calm and gentle demeanor, and enjoy the human touch. They must be able to tolerate children, other animals, crowded public places, and other situations that may be stressful, without becoming distressed or dangerous. They must be content with being petted and handled, sometimes clumsily. There are several different types of therapy dogs. These include Therapeutic Visitation dogs, Disaster Relief Dogs, Facility Therapy Dogs, Animal Assisted Therapy Dogs, and Reading Therapy Dogs. Therapy Dogs are pets, and although they may be certified, they are not trained as professionals in the same sense as guide dogs. (from www.companionanimals.org)

Like most sporting dogs, therapy dogs have friendly, gentle temperaments, and a desire to please people.

When Joanne discovered that the St. John Ambulance organization had a therapy dog program, she decided to attend one of their orientation meetings. No dogs allowed. The session lasted for four hours, and when it ended, Joanne signed Smiley up.

The St. John Ambulance Therapy Program was developed in 1992 as an experimental program based out of Peterborough, Ontario. The program's continuing success is demonstrated by the fact that there are now almost 3,000 dogs with their handlers serving as therapy dog teams across Canada. These units meet thousands of people every year, bringing hope and healing to those in need.

St. John Ambulance has strict rules about the dogs it accepts, and about the conduct of the dogs' handlers. Teams that meet the high standards set by the program visit nursing homes, schools, hospitals, seniors residences, homeless shelters, disaster sites, and hospices. They work with the autistic, the aged, with people in grief, the lonely, people in fear, and those without hope. The dogs are petted, cuddled, and touched as they dispense unconditional love.

Shepherd, Smiley, and Joanne have busy lives!

COMPANIONSHIP, CARE, COMFORT

Therapy dogs can be any breed or size, but there is a process of testing and certification that takes place before a dog can become a therapy dog. There are tiny Chihuahuas and huge Great Danes in the program. Golden and Labrador Retrievers make excellent therapy dogs, for the same reason they make excellent pets. Like most sporting dogs, they have friendly, gentle temperaments, and a desire to please people. Successful dogs need to be eager to meet and connect with everyone.

Some Rottweilers have been found to be good therapy dogs, as have Poodles, Saint Bernards, German Shepherds, and even Greyhounds. Smaller, cuddly dogs like Shih-Tzus, Pugs, Cavalier King Charles Spaniels, Yorkies, and Beagles can be perfect for the role because they can be picked up and loved. Therapy dogs must be calm, affectionate, and not needy.

A few months after her initial meeting, the St. John Ambulance Therapy Program contacted Joanne to ask if she could bring Smiley in for testing. He would work alongside the eight or ten other dogs being tested that day. Joanne was nervous, but acted confidently. Smiley needed to know that this exercise would be a good experience.

The test consisted of several challenges for both Smiley and Joanne – tests that would determine how stable Smiley was. Would Smiley truly enjoy being a therapy dog? Would he improve quality of life for the people he would visit? How did he react to other dogs, to crowds? Was he easily distracted?

At the end of the session, Joanne and Smiley were ushered into a room with all the evaluators present. Joanne was quiet, and Smiley followed the "plop, plop" sound of her flip-flops as she walked over to stand in front of the panel. The lead appraiser had tears in her eyes. Joanne braced herself for the bad news. But no! The tears were tears of joy. Smiley had passed every test with flying colours. He was born to be a superb therapy dog, the woman told Joanne. And on a more personal note, she added, the people Smiley would visit

during his career with St. John Ambulance would be very lucky. Many years later, Joanne herself became a therapy dog evaluator. She found out why the woman cried, and understood how she felt. "Two dogs I accepted into the program have brought me to tears. They, like Smiley, are very special, giving spirits."

Simply petting a therapy dog can decrease stress levels, regulate breathing, and even lower blood pressure. Research has shown that bonding and giving affection releases oxytocin – also known as the "cuddle" or "love" hormone – in both the dog and the human. Yet, surprisingly, many of the people who have been positively affected by Smiley have never placed a hand on his soft fur. Smiley has done something different. He has been able to provide therapy to people all over the world through television and social media.

The end result of kindness
is that it draws people to you.

ANITA RODDICK

Believe you can and you're halfway there.

THEODORE ROOSEVELT

CHAPTER FIVE

SMILEY, THE BLIND THERAPY DOG

Kindness is the language which the deaf can hear and the blind can see.

Mark Twain

By the time Smiley has his St. John Ambulance Therapy Dog bandana tied around his neck and the special red collar with its therapy-dog tags buckled on, he has already turned on his "therapy-dog charm." When arriving for any therapy visit, wherever it may be – library, nursing home, hospital, school – Smiley jumps out of the van, leash in his mouth, and prances to the front door, waving his tail at Joanne to follow. Joanne is convinced Smiley knows how much his spirits lift those of the people he has come to help. When Smiley meets someone in a wheelchair, he will lift his front paws gently up onto the chair's arm so that the person can touch his soft fur. When visiting people who cannot use their arms, Smiley rests his head on a chest or lap, delighting in whatever sound his presence

elicits. Smiley detects happiness and joy in even the loudest and most jarring shrieks.

Joanne believes that Smiley takes his greatest joy in working with children. In addition to his regular evaluation, Smiley had to pass a rigorous child therapy dog examination before he could be certified in this specialty. Every certified child therapy dog must demonstrate extraordinary patience and calm, when presented with large groups of noisy, excited children. Smiley is drawn to the children's joyful energy, their giggly voices, and their questioning minds. "Why is Smiley different?" Joanne is always asked. "Why was he born without eyes? How does he know where he is? Does he bump into things?"

They ask a LOT of questions, and Joanne answers each one because then, she says, "the magic happens." Smiley teaches younger children how to approach a dog, and how dogs like to be petted.

He teaches the older students about not judging others or giving people labels. The children feel comforted by Smiley's presence. He makes each child feel special, and never leaves anyone out. All children worry about being different, but with Smiley, children see that it is beautiful to be different. Smiley senses what is inside a person. He does not need eyes for that.

The best and most beautiful things in the world cannot be seen or even touched – they must be felt with the heart.

HELEN KELLER

Smiley gives his love freely and doesn't judge.

Please Don'T Pre Judge Me, I Am NoT a Druggie oR an alcoholic a Bad guy.

The children can see the happiness in Smiley, despite his past, his struggles, and the fact that he bumped into the desk on his way into the room. They describe him as "loving," "helpful," "inspirational," "heroic," and even "angelic." Joanne tells the children that things might be more difficult for Smiley because he can't see, but that does not stop him from doing everything another dog can do. He just might have to work a little harder.

Smiley regularly visits a local library where he sits with children with special needs and children who have difficulty reading. These

Children are amazed at how happy Smiley is, despite his challenges.

children are able to see that dogs, too, may be born with many of the same problems. They can also see that Smiley has overcome his disabilities, and that he is happy.

Smiley often visits a nursing home where many of the residents are Alzheimer patients. Alzheimer's destroys memory, and most of these people can no longer recognize their own families, although they usually remember their childhood, and sometimes even the family dog. Smiley brings those special canine companions to mind.

Sometimes Joanne and Smiley visit a man named Teddy who lives in a home for adults with physical and mental challenges. Teddy could not speak and was withdrawn because he had no means of communicating with anyone. "One day," Joanne says, "Smiley put his paws up on Teddy's lap. Teddy started smiling and making sounds." Teddy's nurses were astounded. They had never seen him smile before. Now, every time Smiley visits the home, Teddy is the first person he seeks out.

No one ever forgets meeting Smiley. People may feel sad when they first hear his story, but Smiley's "I can do anything" life lesson is what stays with them. Smiley's story of triumph over adversity has now been shared around the world. And, although he has never given his sweet kisses to anyone in Tokyo, or comforted a sick child in Argentina, Smiley still puts hope in these people's hearts.

Named Stouffville's "Citizen of the Year," Smiley wears the Mayor's chain of office.

CHAPTER SIX

SMiLEY, THE CELEBRiTY

The meaning of life is to find your gift.
The purpose of life is to give it away.

Pablo Picasso

Smiley lives in Stouffville, Ontario, a warm, caring community just north of Toronto. Stouffville residents discovered Smiley through articles in their local paper. After reading about this wonderful little dog, people would stop him on the street, recognizing his "smiling face." Everyone wanted to say hello and bask in five minutes of hug therapy from Smiley.

Soon, the local library was inundated with requests for reading sessions with Smiley. He was part of the St. John Ambulance Paws 4 Stories program, which helps children improve their reading skills by reading to a therapy dog. Research studies have repeatedly demonstrated the strong influence a calm and loving canine audience can have on a child's reading abilities and their self-confidence.

As more and more people heard about Smiley through social media, and through word of mouth, his audience began to increase

dramatically. In 2015, Joanne and Smiley were invited to New York as guests on NBC TV's Meredith Vieira talk show. The show's producers offered to fly them from Toronto to New York for the event, but Joanne was determined that Smiley not travel in the airplane's luggage compartment. She had promised Smiley long before that she would never leave him or put him in a situation that might prove frightening or harmful to him. The New York producers really wanted Smiley on their show, and came up with a solution. Smiley was assigned his own seat in the cabin, right next to Joanne and Shepherd! The trip was a success. Both Shepherd and Smiley had fun travelling the moving sidewalk in the airport, and New York's loud and busy traffic kept everyone on their toes.

Smiley is now better than ever after treatment for his "tail end"!

Smiley's media presence was growing and growing. He and Joanne have appeared on CBS News, Global TV, CBC, CNN, Fox, *Inside Edition,* and *BuzzFeed*. Smiley has been written up in the *Huffington Post*, the *Toronto Star*, and the *Washington Post*, among others. Cesar Millan, the famous "Dog Whisperer" has fallen in love with Smiley, as has Archbishop Bishop Desmond Tutu. Smiley has even been to Ottawa to meet Prime Minister Justin Trudeau. Smiley's Facebook page (SmileytheBlindTherapyDog) and his Instagram page (@SmileytheBlindTherapyDog) win him new friends every day. The Royal Canadian Mounted Police awarded Smiley an honorary RCMP Service Dog degree "because he serves his community much the same way RCMP police dogs do."

My mission has always been to save dogs - especially troubled and abandoned dogs. I've dedicated my life to this.
—Cesar Millan

Smiley is getting older now. He is fifteen. One weekend, as the George family prepared to leave the cottage, Joanne noticed that Smiley was not quite his usual sunny self. When it was time to jump into the van, Smiley could not do it. The will was there, but his muscles were weak. The next day, when Joanne and the dogs were out walking, Smiley lost his balance and almost fell over. His hind legs were wobbly and not working right. Joanne phoned her friend, Dr. Tara Edwards, a veterinary rehabilitation specialist, to request an immediate appointment.

Dr. Edwards examined Smiley and rapidly referred him to a neurologist. The specialist was surprised Smiley did not seem to be in any pain. Smiley kept wagging his tail, regardless. The neurologist discovered that the last disk in Smiley's back, the disk closest to his tail, was "compressed," or compacted, a condition which the doctor was certain must have been very painful. When asked how such an injury could occur, the doctor told Joanne that it was probably the result of "overuse" – too much tail wagging!

Smiley was promptly placed on a busy rehabilitation regimen: acupuncture, laser therapy, and deep muscle massage. The results were nothing short of miraculous, and Smiley continued to wag his tail.

His is truly an indomitable spirit.

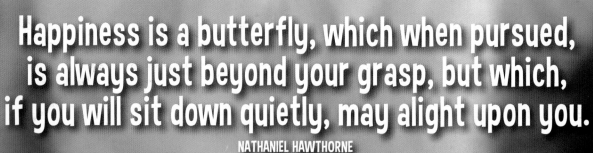

Happiness is a butterfly, which when pursued, is always just beyond your grasp, but which, if you will sit down quietly, may alight upon you.

NATHANIEL HAWTHORNE

WAYS YOU CAN HELP

★ Please visit your local animal shelter when looking for a dog

★ Contact your local shelter or humane society to volunteer your time

★ Donate pet food to a foodbank

★ Consider adopting a special-needs dog

★ Collect food, toys, and blankets to be donated to a rescue organization

★ Foster a dog who is looking for a home

★ Have a garage sale and donate the profits to a rescue organization

★ Care for the dog you have: train him, take him to the veterinarian regularly, and give him love and affection

INDEX